W9-AYF-490

Survive or Die

Survive or Die

**Business Transformation Lessons
Given by the Animal Kingdom**

Ivan Michael Scott

ISBN 978-0-9940706-0-9
Book design by CreateSpace
ISBN: 1512287172
ISBN 13: 9781512287172
Library of Congress Control Number: 2015908134
CreateSpace Independent Publishing Platform
North Charleston, South Carolina

ACKNOWLEDGMENTS

I acknowledge the input of every single person that I have ever met in my life who, whether they know it or not, has had an influence, one way or another, on who I am. I especially acknowledge the help and support of my wife, Merle, who kept me going even through the dark times.

Thanks also to Ilona, Michelle, David, John, Chuck, et al., for their insights and encouragement.

Apologies (and thanks) to Aesop.

Ivan Scott

ivan.scott@winningcareerskills.com

CONTENTS

PREFACE

"Ivan, take this course!"
"Ivan, attend that seminar!"

"All right, Ivan, now that you have all that education in you, go back to what you were doing before and forget it all! Nothing will ever change! We're OK as is."

How many times have you heard statements like these? Being talked to this way is equivalent to opening the door so that you can *see* out, but putting up a locked security gate so that you cannot get out. Eventually, you get sick and tired of these training schemes, so you start looking to join another organization that is more aligned with your career goal of survival.

Or do you?

I was in corporate America for many years, and I became incredibly frustrated about being trained in "how to do" but then not actually being allowed "to do." Why put vice presidents, managers, and others in charge if the plan is to micromanage them and not let them get on with what they are being paid the big bucks to do?

I eventually got out of corporate life. Then, after having my own business for some years, I began to wonder if there were any business-management lessons to be learned from nature's world and whether these could be incorporated into human business models. Since my heritage is African, I put this business book together using various African animal species that are to be viewed as "businesses" in their own right and by using the "markets," "threats," and "strategies" they face as illustrations that I hope will help us understand the basics of business again. I am sure animals the world over face similar challenges of survival to those that humans face.

Each story's challenges and strategies can be analyzed on their own, and parallels to the human business world can be drawn and discussed.

The fables at the beginning of each chapter show that similar survival challenges have been on the minds of animals and people since the fables were written in about 600 BC. The animals in my stories identify their problems and then implement their carefully thought-out solutions to these problems.

It has been fascinating to investigate what animals do to ensure their survival in an extremely hostile environment. Business today is very similar. You have no friends out there—it is a dog-eat-dog, cat-eat-cat, leopard-eat-baboon, company-eat-company world.

Survival is paramount. Lives are at stake.

The animals know.

CHAPTER 1

"Not the roar, but the gait of the lion, leads his pride to run and to follow."
—AFRICAN PROVERB

A TALE OF TWO ENTITIES

The Lion and the Mouse
An Aesop's Fable

A lion was awakened from his sleep by a mouse running over his face. Rising up angrily, he caught the mouse and was about to kill him when the mouse piteously entreated, saying, "If you would only spare my life, I would be sure to repay your kindness." The lion laughed and let him go.

It happened shortly after this that the lion was caught by some hunters who bound him by strong ropes to the ground. The mouse, recognizing his roar, came and gnawed at the rope with his teeth, and set the lion free, exclaiming, "You ridiculed the idea of my ever being able to help you, not expecting to receive from me any repayment of your favor: now you know that it is possible for even a mouse to confer benefits on a lion."

LION LIMITED

The lion's mane rippled and fluffed up in the cool evening air. A gentle breeze came in from the southeast, bringing along the scents and aromas of the Okavango Delta. Large yellow eyes peered intently into the mouth of the soft wind, watching to find the source of the odors. He knew from his extensive experience that even if he did detect something in the quickening gloom, it would most likely be only a trick of his mind, warning him of something he knew was already there—although it was hidden in the shadows and a long way off.

He yawned widely, showing off his magnificently sculpted set of fangs and teeth—tools designed to kill quickly and efficiently. His teeth were a perfect fit for his mouth, and their sharp, jagged edges were designed to rip meat into sizable chunks, which were then swallowed whole. These teeth were a great source of fear to his prey, especially when accompanied by an approaching roar. That warning sound could be heard by all competitors and prey for a distance of up to five miles.

The lion's name was Genghis, a name his parents gave him after seeing how he had assumed the role of protector, leader, and benefactor of his two siblings that had been born eight and seventeen minutes after Genghis had come into the world. With a birth weight of five pounds, he had been larger than his brother, Xerxes, and his sister, Arial. Still five years later, he continued to care for them, using his larger size as leverage.

Genghis had been told by his peers that he was an impressive specimen of the genus *Panthera leo* (lion) and a formidable member of *Felidae* (cat family). At 485 pounds, whenever he walked out onto the open savanna, he projected a physical presence enhanced by the intimidating offer of strength and power that size generally begets. His tawny-colored, tight-fitting coat showed off his well-formed, muscular body to perfection. He worked out regularly; in his line of business, he could not afford to become fat and lazy. Being the leader of his enterprise was all about his being seen as a good example in every way to his pride. This perception earned his leadership every day. His full, dark mane was thick and luxurious. The blond hair on the top of his head was well groomed and clean. These features projected even more inner strength.

Genghis had two genuine smiles. The one for his family showed his love and empathy for them in life's challenges and confirmed his belief and confidence in their being able to do a good team job. The second smile was for his prey, letting them know that there was nothing personal in the death that they were about to experience. The aim of the killing was the pure survival of the pride—it was no place for egos or for a killing just for the sake of sport.

Genghis looked down at his brother, Xerxes, who was lying away to his left, preening himself. Xerxes was waiting for the leader to speak. He knew the pecking order and understood that he was the second-in-charge lion, the COO.

"Brother Xerxes," said Genghis, "it is that time again. The buffalo are near, and we need to get the family fed. Come closer, and let us discuss the strategy of how to get what we need."

The two stood silently for a time and looked out over the surrounding bushveld from the slight promontory that made up their home and base of operations. There was nothing that they knew of that compared to the fiery pinkish-orange of the fading sunset that would soon herald their considered decisions. The sky was dramatic and bold, with quickly ebbing colors that bounced off the stratocumulus clouds that always sneaked up at this time of the day. The clouds were dark and heavy with the life-giving moisture they were prepared to give to the community below. They were groaning and thundering, cracking lightning-fast whips of incandescence as if demanding attention and saying, "We will share with you our gift of rain, whether you want it or not." As the darkness slowly descended, the stars started to make their appearance. The constellations were huge and beautiful, especially the one called Leo.

The two lions talked quietly together, discussing and reviewing the home, habitat, and "business market area" that their pride lived in, known as the Shinde Area portion of the extensive Okavango Delta Swamps, situated in the northwestern corner of Botswana in southern Africa. This incredibly flat, lush, wetland attracted all types of animals from great distances, creating one of Africa's greatest concentrations of wildlife at certain times of the year and offering an ideal food source to lions and other predators. Temperatures in the area fluctuated from extremely hot in the middle of summer, to warm in the winter months.

This was the environment that the lions had to survive or die in. It seemed to be paradise now. Little did they know how this would change for the worse in the months that were to follow. The two leaders put their heads together again and talked more about Lion Limited.

Lion Limited was a typical medium-size, reasonably well-controlled, efficient organization. It was different from your normal pride company in that it had dual leaders at the helm (Genghis and Xerxes) who assumed complete personal responsibility for the performances achieved by their team.

Two years previously, the two nomad lions had stumbled on the Shinde lion pride that was being inefficiently run by a not-so-benevolent dictator named Jason, who was completely stuck in his ways of doing business as usual. Jason had been both deaf and blind to changing circumstances—the competition had become far more aggressive and wanted a more profitable market share for their own stakeholders. Now the new mantra in the savanna was "Survive or Die." These changes meant Jason had become a bad leader suffering from complacency and laziness, resulting in the pride's not expanding in either numbers or talent and not undergoing any suitable training or strategy discussions for years. The result was that the Shinde pride's brand was no longer respected by its competitors or by the prey within its market area. That was the brothers' opportunity!

The coup d'etat by Genghis and Xerxes on Jason had been easy. The old guard was sent on his way, licking his not-so-serious wounds—after all, two to one in a fight had not been fair odds. It had then taken a week to convince the rest of the pride that their new leaders did actually have their best interests at heart.

The hierarchical structure of Lion Limited after the takeover, comprised the two males—Genghis as CEO (long-term strategy and planning) and Xerxes as COO (operations)—and seven lionesses, each with her own business portfolio in addition to fulfilling the main job description of hunter-provider. There were no cubs—they had all been killed by the new leaders, as is the lion custom in takeovers. The pride under the previous regime had been totally demoralized, unsettled, and torn, but after the two brothers had won the right to run the Shinde pride, all seven females delivered with eleven new cubs being born, thereby making a substantial investment in the pride's long-term survival.

Lionesses are the core members of a lion pride, and they are all collectively bound by one major purpose—to hunt, so that all of the members of the pride can eat. In summer, they hunt the large African buffalo abundant in the Shinde area of the Okavango but only available to them for half of the year. After the rains stop and the grasses are depleted, the buffalo leave for greener pastures. However, while they are still in the area, they feast on the lush vegetation of the islands and flood-plains, while the lions feed on them.

Buffalo were the most desirable, but also the most dangerous, prey to the Shinde lions—desirable because the meat from a fifteen-hundred-pound buffalo fed the entire pride for up to a week, and dangerous because their formidably sharp horns could inflict a fatal wound to even the biggest lion. The seven Shinde lionesses had learned this early in their hunting careers. Genghis and Xerxes trained the lionesses over and over again, honing their hunting and killing skills to perfection, utilizing a team environment.

"The day after tomorrow, we must send six of the lionesses out after the Bedwe buffalo herd," Genghis said to Xerxes. "Malkai must stay behind and protect the cubs and our backs from a possible attack by the hyenas or marauding Moremi lions, while the rest of us must have our attention focused on the killing. The Moremis will take over our territory in a heartbeat if we let our guard down even for a minute."

"I agree," said Xerxes. "However, we need to take Shemsi aside beforehand for some intense training from both of us. She seems to have lost a bit of vigor and enthusiasm of late, which is starting to be noticed by the others and is affecting the pride's morale. We need to realign ourselves regularly with our mission so that we stay lean and mean in order to achieve our team's goals."

"Absolutely!" said Genghis. "Set up the training with us for seven o'clock tomorrow morning for two hours. We will execute the Alpha Plan after that, scheduling the hunt to start at noon in the high heat of the following day, when the buffalo are exhausted from standing in the blazing sun. They will not expect our attack then. We must get as much rest as we can that morning to conserve our energy so that we can easily outrun and outwit them. We will also investigate them using the Alpha Plan, which these buffalo are not very familiar with. Also, both of us must be very confident in our leadership, and we need to be prepared to assist, when required, in every way possible to assure the hunt's success."

Alpha was a plan that had been developed by the two leaders in close concert with their team of lionesses over the past two years and which had been modified regularly in order to accommodate the ever-changing competitive landscape. It was part of a larger strategy that included two alternative plans. With the current Alpha Plan, the leader lions took only a very small part in the hunt, leaving it to the lionesses who were far better suited for the plan's execution. The males monitored from the sidelines, observing to see if there were any areas in which the game plan fell down or any improvements they needed to make for the strategy to be more efficient and effective the next time that the plan was utilized.

To effectively execute the Alpha Plan, the two leaders would identify and follow a buffalo herd for at least one full day, constantly watching and sizing up their options, choosing some potential targets, and studying the movements and positions of these targets within the herd. The lionesses and cubs would be there, too—but hidden. On their slow march in search of food, the buffalo never noticed more than one or two lions, with the result that they generally did not see or seem to appreciate the looming threat. Eventually, the pride singled out one buffalo that they would separate from the herd. They usually chose this to be a mother, concentrating their combined power on bringing her down and ignoring her newborn calf. Injured mothers were even better targets.

Inevitably, the time would come to attack. One of the male lions, together with a supporting female, would act as decoy predators, chasing random targets so as to fragment and confuse the herd. The balance of the lionesses would then all attack the intended target in unison. Using all of her strength, the lead female for the day would suffocate the animal by getting a good bite on its throat and crushing its windpipe. She would then clamp her mouth over the victim's nose and mouth while the other pride members held it down and broke its spine.

That was the plan.

The plan was implemented.

The plan worked.

The plan was used often.

Later that year, however, the Shinde pride saw its fortunes take a turn for the worse as the Okavango dealt out one of its harshest seasons ever. During the summer, while the buffalo roamed in their territory, the pride was guaranteed regular meals. But by the end of May, the rains ceased, which marked the start of a period of extreme hardship for the lions. The buffalo moved out of the Shinde area, looking for more nutritious grasses. They were replaced by breeding herds of elephants which arrived from the surrounding Kalahari Desert and spread out into the forests and floodplains in the heart of the Delta. The elephants came because the water in the surrounding desert had dried up and the vegetation had shriveled away. Shinde offered them permanent water.

As the pride's cubs grew going into the winter, their demand for food grew as well. The pressure thus increased on the lionesses to provide more meat, more often for the pride. Even Genghis and

Xerxes, who were used to waiting on the sidelines, were regularly called into action. Efficient hunting required a total team effort, and the many seasons of taking down buffalo had taught each pride member exactly what they had to do to ensure success. However, that expertise had made the Shinde lions vulnerable since they were totally dependent on dining on a single product—buffalo. There were other prey choices around them, but hunting giraffe, for example, demanded a completely different strategy. Giraffes were more alert than buffalo and would spot the pride and the clumsy cubs from far away, giving the lions little or no chance to strike. Giraffes are also not as gentle as they look—they can deliver a kick so vicious that it can knock even Genghis unconscious or even kill him. So, while the buffalo were still in the Shinde territory, the lions concentrated their efforts on hunting only them. But the season had changed, and as the buffalo depleted each field of grass, they moved onto the next field, each day a little more distant from the Shinde lions' center of operations.

The Shinde lions were halted in their relentless pursuit of food as the seventh lioness had given birth to two more cubs—swelling the number of youngsters to a challenging thirteen that still needed to be fed even when the Shinde area was at its most desperate. All the while, the lions' main prey slipped further from their grasp. Meanwhile, as the buffalo left, the elephants arrived. Elephants are less fussy eaters than buffalo and can make do with the coarser grasses and reeds that the buffalo leave behind. The two species crossed paths—one came for water, the other left for sweeter grasses. The lions lost their main buffalo food source—elephants were not on their menu, at least not yet.

Then there was the border of the Shinde territory, an invisible line that the Shinde lions would not cross, because another pride, the Moremis, ruled on the other side. But this didn't stop the buffalo from crossing though. The Shinde pride would not follow the buffalo across since moving their cubs into enemy territory would be far too dangerous. The group thus deferred to the Moremis and remained inside its own market area, while the last of the buffalo left the Shinde area for the rest of the season.

The pride kept moving about, looking for anything they could chase down and eat. They actively ignored the elephants because they were large and very difficult to hunt and kill. Eventually, some of the cubs started exhibiting signs of weakness. The pride couldn't rest for long periods and had to travel extensively in search of food, which took a terrible toll on its smallest members. However, the only prey the pride could see now were elephants, and they eventually started looking at them with interest. With nothing else to eat, the lions needed to reconsider their strategy to ensure their survival. Too tired and too weak to keep up with their mothers, the cubs were starving—with six of them having already died. Only the fittest would have a fighting chance, but without food, they would have no chance at all. The surviving cubs tried to drink from their mothers, but the starving lionesses' milk had gone dry. The balance of the pride constantly scanned the horizons for something edible, but saw nothing but elephants traveling in tight groups.

Lion Limited was failing badly in its core purpose of sustaining life. What would the pride have to do to ensure their survival in this changed and much more hostile environment? They finally realized that when their actual survival was at stake, a new strategy needed to be developed and implemented. They had to change. Alternative prey had to be found.

Eventually the pride's persistence in following the elephants, constantly looking out for opportunities paid off. The lionesses noted that young elephants were unaccustomed to danger and were vulnerable. Sure enough, a five-year-old elephant male had lost his way, and his trumpeting cries went unheard by his family. He was unable to outrun the lions, and his tusks were too small to be used as defensive weapons. The lionesses attacked and drove the four-thousand-pound animal to the ground and held him down. Although they were expert buffalo killers, the lionesses had never tried to kill an elephant before. Their efforts were clumsy and initially not very effective—their teeth couldn't penetrate his one-and-a-half-inch thick skin, and his neck was far too wide to effectively grab hold of and strangle. They attacked the softer, more vulnerable spots. Without a muzzle to suffocate him, they held on to his trunk, but they were unable to kill the elephant in the traditional buffalo-kill way—so they started to eat him alive. The first taste of meat after almost a month of starvation revived their stamina, and they relished every mouthful. Three times the size of a buffalo, the young elephant kept the pride well fed for days, introducing them to a new food product.

Over the next few weeks, the lions worked diligently to refine their newfound elephant-killing techniques. They persisted, and, in that dry season that had started so disastrously, killing elephants turned from being an act of desperation to becoming a new way of life. Out of the original thirteen cubs, seven had survived, and they dined heartily together with the nine adults. Genghis and Xerxes were well pleased with how Lion Limited had managed to turn itself around in the face of incredible adversity. Change, persistence, and training had paid great dividends. They were again a viable entity.

By the end of the winter and under the washed-out skies of an excruciatingly hot October, wave after wave of tired elephants had moved through the Shinde lions' territory. The herds had had their fill of life-giving water, but the scrappy vegetation had offered them little nutritional value. Mothers and calves had grown weak, and some of the older calves had strayed and gotten lost. The lionesses, of course, had exploited these opportunities. For the pride, this had then become a season of in-dulgence—in one month, they had killed five ele-phants, ensuring their pride's survival and teaching the cubs the ways of the new hunt.

During the most desperate Okavango season in decades, just over half of the cubs had survived. This was a better than normal survival rate, due to the Shinde lions' ability to change their hunting model. The spread of fresh, sweet grass lured the buffalo herds back into the Shinde territory. The li-ons eagerly watched their favorite food arrive—fif-teen hundred pounds of buffalo with a reasonably soft hide to pierce, and a short snout easy to smoth-er. During the next six months of rain, the cubs learned to hunt buffalo by trial and error. This was not as easy as their parents made it seem, although they became experts soon enough after extensive training. During the summer months, the constant supply of buffalo meat turned the young lions into strong, eighteen-month-old, self-sufficient predators, and they became part of an efficient hunting pride, sixteen strong. The youngsters emulated their parents' every move—learning when to strike, when to wait, when to hide, and when to explode into the open. As sub-adults, they were old enough to test their strengths in their pride's formidable battles. They strode confidently up front with their parents and attacked side by side with them.

Genghis summed up in a very succinct way one evening while the Shinde pride was lying in their den. "In this ever-changing landscape of prosperity and hardship, our pride has finally found stability. With Xerxes and I in command and a healthy number of youngsters to ensure the pride's existence, we have come full circle in the business of survival. From our desperation sprang our collective ingenuity and creativity. We switched prey to win the war waged by the harshest environment we have ever endured. We experienced the need for new products, a realization of the necessity of well-trained team members and successors. We had a total and fully committed belief in our cause. Our culture adapted. The lessons of survival have been learned. We have changed—and have survived!"

he said proudly. The pride was in full agreement with this.

Life in the Okavango will always be unpredictable, and the grown cubs will one day have to face that by themselves. Soon their fathers will expel them, and they will have to form prides of their own. The struggle of one season was over, but the struggle for survival is never ending. The Shinde lions will always be a pride in battle.

However, the strategy and leadership of Lion Limited had worked—the pride would now survive.

LEADERS LAUNCH FORTH BEFORE SUCCESS IS CERTAIN.

CHAPTER 2

"Elephants are symbols of might and memory, harmony and patience, power and compassion."
—LYALL WATSON

A LARGE AND SMALL TALE

The Mouse and the Elephant
A Modified Aesop's Fable

An elephant was bitten by a mouse and, angered by the wound, tried to capture him. But the mouse reached his hole in safety. Though the elephant dug into the walls with his tusks, he tired before he could rout out the mouse and, crouching down, went to sleep outside the hole. The mouse peeped out, crept furtively up his flank, and again bit the elephant before retreating to his hole. The elephant rose up, and not knowing what to do, was sadly perplexed. At which point, the mouse said, "The great do not always prevail. There are times when the small and lowly are the strongest to do mischief."

ELEPHANT ENTERPRISES

The watering hole was large in area and about six feet deep at its center. It contained a lake of mud-colored water, and it was generally kept filled over the rainy season by a small tributary of the nearby Thaoge River. Crocodiles floated around in the water pretending they were dead logs, with birds perching on their backs, using the crocodiles as resting places.

A herd of twelve African elephants were at the water hole drinking, spraying one another with water, bathing, or acting as lookouts. The herd was made up of its matriarch: Eliva, six other females, four calves ranging from one to ten years of age, and a young fourteen-year-old bull named Mufta.

Eliva was the oldest and largest elephant of the herd. This qualified her to be its matriarch, a position she had held for the past fifteen of her forty-five years of age. Her pet name for her group was Elephant Enterprises, which she tried to run while following sound "business-type" principles. Eliva was standing on a small knoll, acting as a lookout over the water hole, having an unrestricted 360-degree vista of at least one-half mile in all directions. Kalifa, her eldest daughter, was standing beside her, thus doubling the number of eyes watching for possible predators.

"My dear Kalifa," Eliva said, "I had a dream last night. I dreamed that we elephants are faced with two major threats, and if we do not do something soon about them, our very survival will be at stake."

"Go on, Mother," said Kalifa. "I am listening."

"The first threat that I dreamed about was that a substantial climate change was coming soon globally and that key portions of our habitat will become significantly hotter and drier. This will result in much poorer foraging conditions for us, threatening us with starvation and making us physically weak," said Eliva.

"This climate change will also affect the rest of the animal kingdom and will have the result in making predators more desperate in their search for new prey. We, the elephants, will most certainly be targeted much more by lions as time goes on. In order to ensure our survival in the future, we need to be very clear about what it is that we have to do. What we are doing now and what we have done in the past is no longer a sufficient enough guarantee for us," said Eliva. "The sleeping elephant now needs to be awakened!"

"I hear you very clearly, Mother. What is the second threat?" asked Kalifa.

"The second threat is from the humans wanting our tusks as ornaments, and about this, I have very little idea of what to do. They have cars and guns, and we are big and slow. The only thing I can think is to always be extremely vigilant, communicate their presence to one another extremely efficiently, and move as quickly away from them as we can whenever we become aware of them in our area. We must avoid them at all costs," said Eliva. "This must become part of our culture."

The two elephants walked together down to the watering hole and stood at its edge. Eliva looked at her reflection in the water. She and Kalifa were both about 14 feet tall and each weighed nearly fourteen thousand pounds. Elephants need up to four hundred pounds of food per day which, as she had told Kalifa before, placed enormous demands on their delicate surrounding environment.

"Of paramount importance in our fight for survival is firstly to have discipline in our herd," said Eliva to Kalifa, referencing Mufta.

Mufta was a delinquent juvenile bull who had grown up without any solid male role models. This had led to a naughtiness and bad behavior that disrupted the herd. Mufta had an inflated opinion of his own importance to the world and tried to demonstrate this at every opportunity.

"We have to call on Jamba to help with the discipline and training process, starting with Mufta," said Eliva. "We need to be unified to have a strong team. Mufta's bad choices have made a great impression on his cousins, and we have to immediately reeducate him and all of the calves in the correct ways. Jamba must come in and assume the role of stepfather in our family."

Jamba was a mature bull elephant who generally lived a lone existence away from any herds but was periodically called in by some of them to act as a sort of "contracting consultant." He assisted with any challenges that herds might identify and could not effectively handle themselves in-house. He was well respected within the elephant community and performed his requested tasks well. Disciplining the youngsters would not be a problem for him.

"Our next task is to forage for and consume our food more efficiently as a group. We must not be wasteful of the food sources, and we must look . after and care for them. We must also remember where we have eaten before and avoid going through those places again before they have a chance to regenerate. When we do enter a new area, we need to take the full one hundred percent of what is there, in the smallest possible area, during the time that we are there. This we must do in a controlled manner to conserve the resources," Eliva explained.

"Then we need to stay within easy walking distance of water. We need to know where all of the reliable watering areas are and which of those are available to us in our territory. We must conserve these water resources for ourselves for the future.

"The last thing that we have to do is to maintain our herd between twelve and twenty members, including calves. Any fewer than twelve and we will lose our status and not be able to defend ourselves effectively if attacked by predators. Any more than twenty will make our enterprise more difficult to manage efficiently. I believe that any increase in numbers over and above twenty must be very carefully considered, and if done, the process should be slow and sure," Eliva said. "I believe that this overall strategy falls into the realm of using common sense, which we have not used very much of lately. Set the wheels in motion, Kalifa!"

"Immediately, Mother," said Kalifa.

LEADERS MOVE OTHERS TO ACTION, COMMUNICATE PERSUASIVELY, AND STRENGTHEN CONFIDENCE.

CHAPTER 3

"You don't need a title to be a leader."
—MARK SANBORN

A TALE OF RELEVANCE

Perfect
By Ivan Scott (1952–)

The first turtle emerges from the blue
Takes a breath of flawless air
Lays her eggs in an un-spoilt, pristine beach
Forty babies will emerge and return to Atlantis
Nature is perfect

The first rhinoceros walks the plain
Takes his steps on virgin ground
Meets with the second rhinoceros
Produces a baby in Eden, safely
Nature is perfect

The first cheetah appears on the veld
A beautiful, majestic animal
It kills only for food and survival
It is in balance
Nature is perfect

CHEETAH CORPORATION

Faster, faster—I must go faster! This Thomson's gazelle must be the all-time champion sprinter of his species. Why the heck did I choose him to attack today? I have never had to chase one that is nearly as fast as this. I must be doing at least sixty-five miles per hour; he is just ahead of me, and I am not gaining. Left and right, right and left! Run in a straight line, you twit! Actually, I am the twit…I must back off now—I am too tired to chase anymore. We must have run at least three-quarters of a mile, and I am completely tapped out. I am panting so heavily. I don't want to suffer a heart attack or stroke. There must be an easier and more efficient way to do this. It is your lucky day, gazelle. I will get you next time.

Whew! With these thoughts racing through his mind, the cheetah quickly slowed himself down and came to a complete stop, generating a cloud of red, African dust.

This was Felix, a magnificent male specimen of the extremely rare king cheetah genus. He had just had another success taken away from him due to his overconfidence and arrogance in his method of chasing down his prey. He was only successful in his hunt these days about 50 percent of the time, and he considered himself to be one of the top performers of his kind. He, however, was quickly becoming aware that this was not the type of return that he wanted for the incredible individual efforts that he and his coalition were putting in just to survive in the business of life.

At four years of age, Felix was the oldest of Cheetah Corporation, a group of three male and, occasionally, two female king cheetahs. The males, as was the custom in the cheetah world, made up the core of the coalition, and the females came in generally only when mating was required. They stayed around then for only a short period of time, preferring a solitary female existence to a social family one. The females returned to the group only after the cubs were born, for extended periods of up to eighteen months.

Felix was a very regal-looking, strikingly hand-some, 170-pound animal. His chest was deep, and his waist was narrow. His coarse, short fur was a golden tan color, covered with black round spots.

He sported the three typical king cheetah black stripes all the way along his back from the nape of his neck to the beginning of his tail. The black "tear" marks running from the corner of Felix's eyes down along the sides of his nose to his mouth gave him a mystical look and his body rippled with muscles that he kept in fine trim. If he had been in the human corporate business world, his dress would have been almost perfect.

Felix wanted to be known as a "class act" and be an example that the other cheetahs in his coalition would aspire to become, and that other cheetah coalitions would have great respect for. He suspected that his competitors survived in this very unforgiving world by knowing how to change and adapt quickly in the ever-fluid landscape of life, which had long-since evolved past the more cutthroat tactics that had once ruled the day. The challenge was getting to know how to survive and thrive in this dog-eat-dog and cat-eat-cat climate.

Felix had made his home territory in the 7,580-square-mile Kruger National Park in northeastern South Africa. He had laid claim to 150 of those square miles as his territory for his coalition, and he was prepared to fight any other cheetah coalition leader to the death in order to preserve his claim.

Felix lay down in the shade cast by an old, tannin-rich, very thorny, and beautifully exotic acacia tree. As he recovered from the unsuccessful exertion that he had just undertaken, he reflected on what was needed to achieve optimal survival for both himself and his coalition. As a group, the kill rate needed to be increased as all of the members had to be fed. He knew now that they needed to have a leader, and there and then he made the commitment to be that leader. He knew instinctively what was needed to achieve their goals. A huge amount of change was required, but he also knew that this was a one-step-at-a-time process in order not to scare the other members of his coalition.

Felix realized that to earn leadership, one had to lead by example. Honesty, integrity, respect, and truthfulness were nonnegotiable. Trust was paramount. As their leader, he had to lay out practical and attainable goals and strategies both simply and clearly. He also knew that if the coalition did not change, it would experience a downward spiral, finally resulting in their eventual starving extinction.

The first goal that Felix made for himself and the coalition was to increase the hunting success rate from the poor 50 percent that was now being achieved, up to about 65 percent—an ambitious, but obtainable improvement, he was convinced.

He was sure that this would result in a major turn-around in their fortunes and go a long way to assisting in and ensuring their survival.

The second goal that Felix set was to evaluate what alternative prey products were available in their territory and to focus on those that were most easily obtained with the least effort—a sort of low-hanging fruit. Those animals that were slower and easier to catch and had a good nutritional value would be very high on the list. Also minimum size and availability were very important, like vast herds of springbok, impalas, and Grant's gazelles, as well as young wildebeests and zebras. Hares and guinea fowl were included only as a very last resort as too much effort was expended on them for far too little return.

The third goal was to immediately introduce into the coalition a team culture concept. Solitary hunting was wasteful, but if all three males hunted together in tag-team style, success rates would undoubtedly go up. There were, however, some operating strategy details that were needed to be sorted out in order to successfully achieve this goal.

Felix decided that three goals were enough for the present time, and he walked back to the den to inform the others of his proposal. He needed complete buy-in from all of the members of the coalition in order to guarantee success. He would also discuss details with them that would ensure a workable and successful plan. He thought how he would do this, as he walked.

As his first priority, he would have to make a team out of the coalition, but he knew that this would not be an easy task. Sirius and Lightning, the other two male cheetahs, did not have the most accommodating personalities and were suspicious of everything that he said and did. They were afraid of any change to the status quo in case it would lead to their having to do far more for less return.

Felix proceeded to lay out his plan to Sirius and Lightning as well as to the females, Shari and Athena, who were also present, each suckling two three-month-old cubs. He explained to them the utmost importance of working as a team. After all, they all did have the diverse skills and resources necessary that when used in a co-ordinated way would definitely accomplish their goals. Both Shari and Athena had welcomed Felix's overtures unconditionally. The amounts of meat coming in over the last three months had not been enough, and everyone in the coalition seemed to be constantly hungry and weak as a result. The hungrier each member got, the more selfish each became, eventually only killing for themselves, with the coalition suffering overall as a result. The cubs were not growing sufficiently in size, nor were they improving mentally as they should have been, as their mothers' milk was lacking in both quantity and quality. This lack of food had led to the group's taking cutbacks and austerity measures, such as rationing. Anything that could be done to improve the situation was to be welcomed. Sirius and Lightning, the males, were more circumspect since they had experienced similar talks before in another coalition, and those plans had not been carried through to completion. They started discussing it between themselves after Felix had laid out his vision, and they promised their answer to the group within an hour.

"Felix, we have discussed and argued the merits of your plan between us, and we have come to the following conclusion," Sirius, the bigger of the two, said. "We are intelligent enough to understand that if you don't get absolute buy-in and support from every one of us, the strategy will be doomed to failure, and we will all lose in what will become a 'spiral to death.' Lightning and I are both prepared to throw in our lot unequivocally, with you becoming our recognized leader, and give it our all. Your vision now must become our vision. Let us now work out the details—this is a fight for survival that we will win only if we are an effective team."

Felix felt as though a huge weight had been removed from his shoulders, and he thanked them for their words and positive support. He promised them that he would work tirelessly for the good of the coalition and not for his own ego. The five cheetahs then sat around in a circle and worked out their "business plan," including the all-important Strengths/ Weaknesses/ Opportunities/ Threats (SWOT) analysis.

Within three days, the group had moved through phase one and was on phase two of the new strategy. Phase one had been completed on day two and had involved the three male cheetahs doing a complete, formal, on-site survey of the types of prey animals that were available within their territory. This included finding out what number and sizes the animals were (volume); their nutritional advantages (value); their defenses (*strengths*); their running speeds (*weaknesses*); how attentive they were to the danger of being hunted (*opportunity*); which other predators might be interested in hunting them (*threats*); and how far they were from the coalition's home base (logistics). The cheetahs had spent the previous two days conscientiously surveying the market before finally deciding on the second evening that the nearby herds of Grant's gazelles would be their targets of choice for the next three months. This decision would be re-evaluated after that, based on the results that had been achieved.

The advantages of choosing the Grant's gazelle as the prey of choice by the cheetah coalition were - their relatively short height of up to thirty-six inches; their bulk weights from 110 to 180 pounds each; their maximum running speed of a relatively slow forty-five miles per hour; and their preference for grazing in open grasslands. A typical herd generally numbered twenty to thirty animals – a good minimum number to attack.

The first targeted herd of Grant's gazelles had been ensconced in shrub land about two and a half miles away for the past three days. It didn't seem to have been molested by any predators during that time, and the gazelles were probably in a relaxed state of awareness. In among them were three older and larger males, with one exhibiting an injury to his front right leg by way of a slight limp. This was the animal that the cheetahs had targeted to be their first kill.

Felix, Sirius, and Lightning left the den at sunrise on the third day and moved at a fast and silent pace, arriving after twenty minutes travel at the area where they knew the gazelles were camped. There they were—all twenty-seven of them, with the target animal conveniently standing apart and a little to the right of the herd.

The cheetahs' plan called for both Lightning and Felix to go one-quarter mile past the target animal and then spread themselves one-quarter mile apart, in the direction they wanted to chase the gazelle. Sirius, who was the initial chaser, would remain back and close up very quietly to within thirty yards of the target and wait for the signal to initiate the attack. When all three cheetahs were all in position, Lightning, being the middle-positioned, would then give the signal to begin the attack by way of two loud, high-pitched barks (or chirps), which had a singsong, birdlike sound to them. Sirius would then break cover and start the chase without having any responsibility to actually catch or kill the prey. After the first quarter-mile segment of the chase, he would defer to Lightning, who would then take over with a fresh set of legs before finally handing the chase over to Felix who would then run the gazelle down and deliver the coup de grace.

The signal came, and the plan was carried out flawlessly according to the strategy. Felix easily caught up with and tripped the tired gazelle. He proceeded to suffocate it by biting it on the underside of its throat, and he waited for Sirius and Lightning to catch up to assist him in killing it, which they both did. The body of the dead gazelle was then triumphantly dragged back to the coalition's den, where it was eagerly consumed by all members with a great deal of excitement and celebration.

The new strategy was strictly stuck to over the following three months, and a kill was made on average every three days showing an 80 percent success rate, which greatly exceeded the goal target of 65 percent. News of Cheetah Corporation's successes quickly spread across the savanna, and soon many well-qualified king cheetahs made overtures and applications to join their organization, appreciating the value that would accrue to them personally by being part of such a successful enterprise. However, Felix's group was so confident now with their working model that they could afford to accept the crème de la crème of the applicants. They welcomed two new male cheetahs into their coalition during the next three months after interviewing them twice each.

The corporation held its official evaluation meeting after the initial three-month period had expired and the members decided to entrench this new basic business model as they now used it. The slogan of "survive or die" became the more palatable "survive and prosper." They now had a very well-thought-out plan that worked!

A success story indeed for Cheetah Corporation.

LEADERS ARE SPECIFIC IN WHAT THEY EXPECT.

CHAPTER 4

*"The fruit on the ground belongs
to all, but the one in the tree
is for she who can climb."*
—SHONA PROVERB

A TALE OF TWO MORE ENTITIES

The Baboons and Their Mother
A Modified Aesop's Fable

The baboon, it is said, has two young ones at each birth. The mother fondles one and nurtures it with the greatest care but hates and neglects the other. It happened once that the favored young one that was caressed and loved was smothered by the too-great affection of the mother, and it died. The despised one was nurtured and reared in spite of the neglect to which it was exposed.

Best intentions will not always ensure success.

BABOON BROKERAGE

"Let me see now," said Barabbas to his mother. "We have highly engaged, motivated, and loyal members in our troop—all energized and passionate about what they do. They are a team, albeit a reasonably large team of fifty-five members, all of whom understand that if everyone in the group pulls his or her weight in the common direction of your vision, then we as a group will be guaranteed survival and growth."

Barabbas was a fine example of a Chacma baboon, the savanna species of baboon. Chacmas form large groups, or troops, composed of dozens or sometimes even hundreds of members. They govern themselves by a complex system that fascinates all other animal species and have evolved over thousands of years to enjoy a strict matriarchal hierarchy. Perfect communication with complete understanding is paramount in their world. This is because confrontations, or ranking challenges, have a very wide impact on the troop as a whole.

Barabbas was the typical baboon opportunistic omnivore and selective feeder. He ate berries, seeds, roots, leaves, and grasses, as well as insects, birds, fish, rabbits, and small antelope. Baboon diet preferences very much determine where baboons are found in the wild, which then becomes very important information to their predators. Although the main predators of baboons are humans, they also struggle against crocodiles, lions, hyenas, and leopards. This was the market place that the group of baboons, that Barabbas was part of, was in. They called themselves "Baboon Brokerage" and were resident in the 250-square-mile Sabi Sand Game Reserve in northern South Africa.

Baboon behavior varies greatly depending on the social ranking within the troop, and serious fights between males are not unusual. Males also try to win the friendship of females by grooming them, helping care for their young, or supplying them with food, which then generally leads to a more relaxed and trusting environment within the greater group. New members (infants) are generally weaned after about one year. Adult females are the primary caretakers, teachers, and mentors of these infants, and they accept a collective responsibility for the training of the infants in the culture of baboon-hood. Having a very well understood succession plan was very important to the leaders of Baboon Brokerage so that the survival of their species would be guaranteed.

Sixteen-year-old Barabbas, even though he stood thirty-four inches tall and weighed a muscular ninety-one pounds, knew that he was not the leader of the group. He deferred that title to his twenty-seven-year-old mother, Elvira, who had been, for the last seven years, a strict disciplinarian in the running of the troop. She was regarded as a "benevolent CEO" who viewed the world as a challenge with numerous opportunities for improvement that were available to be grasped. She always preached optimism, even when faced with what were sometimes seen by others as insurmountable obstacles.

Wednesday arrived—a day that started like so many other early summer days in the African savanna, holding the not-so-welcome promise of heat, heat, and more heat.

That was the day Barabbas died.

Barabbas awoke at his usual time of sunup and slid down from his regular perch in the troop's baobab tree and into the tall grass of the bushveld beneath. He did this in his very normal and casual way as he did every day. Little did he suspect or anticipate that a leopard had taken note of his habits, and had been waiting patiently below for two hours for just such a mistake to be made. And what a mistake it was. *Wham!* Barabbas did not know what had hit him as the leopard attacked. His skull and doglike muzzle collapsed in on themselves under the tremendous pressure exerted by the leopard's extremely powerful jaws. The explosive crack immediately awoke the rest of the troop in the tree, sending them into paroxysms of fear and excitement when they realized what the cause of the sound was. It was all over in a few seconds, and the leopard dragged the body of Barabbas quickly into the shadows of the morning and away from the shrieking and screaming troop.

Barabbas's death devastated his mother, Elvira. How could they have all been so stupid? She then realized that her troop had mistakenly understood what they needed to survive; they had become complacent, negligent, habitual, and arrogant in believing that Baboon Brokerage had complete control of its safety and environment. Elvira had not seen the warning signs that they had become targets ready for picking. It had been reported that other baboon troops had suffered similar occurrences, but these had been discounted as isolated incidents not really worthy of investigation. Elvira's troop had rested on their laurels and had not exhibited the slightest paranoia about their competitors and predators, which an excellent organizational leadership should have taught. She had to do something about this state of affairs; otherwise Baboon Brokerage would not survive – it would fade into history. She had put too much effort into it for this to happen. There had to be a re-thinking of every item of business and life that they presently undertook, from the smallest to the largest. Each activity had to be broken down, studied for the value that it brought, and then either kept and built on, or rejected and discarded as having no benefit. A meeting of all of the minds had to be called immediately. Every baboon would be affected by whatever decisions were made at the meeting, and input was required from each troop member. The killing had to stop! Chaos would ensue if nothing was done after such a traumatic event. Introducing the changes needed in the organization would not be easy to undertake but drastic steps were required.

Later that day, all adult members of the troop convened an emergency meeting to discuss what had happened that morning and what steps the group as a whole needed to take so that it would not happen again.

Elvira, as Baboon Brokerage's leader, assumed the chair and opened the meeting with the following words:

"My fellow team members, today we experienced a devastating blow to our family—my son,

Barabbas, was taken from us. While this may seem like a disaster to some of us, we must not despair, and we must overcome this setback with courage, fortitude, vision, and resolve.

"We must have the *courage* to face the truths as to the reason why it occurred. For this, I, as your leader, take and accept full responsibility for Barabbas's death. We need to find the root cause of the incident, and we must not rest until we have done so.

"We must have the *fortitude* to remain calm and carry on with the day-to-day business of ensuring the survival of our troop. This involves, firstly, each of you attending to your immediate family's living needs and, secondly, then attending to our wider Baboon Brokerage's stability needs.

"We must develop and realize a *vision* for Baboon Brokerage and plan for it to help us march into the future as a united team, meeting its challenges with the utmost confidence and using all of the tools available to us.

"Finally, we must *all* accept our part of the responsibility for efficiently achieving our stated goal of troop survival at all costs. We must be absolutely *resolute* in this, and we must know and do whatever it takes, both morally and ethically, to achieve this.

"By subscribing to this, we have no choice but to succeed! However, in order for this plan to work, I need you *all* on board. We have experienced a major failure, but we can make a comeback.

"Are you with me?"

They were.

A LEADER IS A SERVANT.

CHAPTER 5

*"A tree is straightened
when it is young."*
—OVAMBO AFRICAN PROVERB

A FURTHER TALE

The Hyena and the Lion
A Modified Aesop's Fable

A hyena, having stolen a young wildebeest from its mother, was carrying him off to her lair. A lion met her on the path and seized the youngster from her. Standing at a safe distance, the hyena exclaimed, "You have unrighteously taken that which was mine from me!"

To which the lion jeeringly replied, "It was righteously yours, eh? A gift from a friend perhaps?"

HYENA HABITAT

"*Who-oop! Who-oop! Who-oop! Who-oop! Who-oop! Who-oop!*" These were the spontaneous and typical sounds made by adult spotted (or laughing) hyenas. Sounds that were made for no particular reason apart from just letting other hyena clans know that they existed.

Hera, the large female hyena making the sounds, was standing next to the impressive giant baobab tree near the Kenya-Tanzania border of the 5,700-square-mile Serengeti National Park. She looked a little puzzled and bewildered, wondering why on earth she was actually making the sounds as there was no particular reason to do so. She suddenly felt a bit stupid with respect to the impression she must be projecting while who-ooping. She was unkempt and exuded a not-so-very pleasant odor. She stood with her head bent down and with her mouth opened slightly, all the while drooling and looking at nothing in particular.

Physically, Hera exhibited the typical hyena characteristics of having a strong, well-developed neck and front quarters, with hindquarters that rounded down, restricting any attackers from being able to get a decent hold on her. Her head was wide and flat on top and she had a blunt muzzle and rounded ears. Her large and extremely powerful jaw muscles, together with her bone-crushing premolars and carnassial teeth, allowed her to crack and break open even the very largest bones of her various victims. She needed at least twenty pounds of meat per meal, so the sizes and amounts of kills had to be made according to the numbers of the hunting party's clan for survival. She had the hide of a typical member of her species. Her fur was short, and of a pale yellow-brown color, with an irregular pattern of one-inch-diameter roundish, black spots all over, except on her throat and chest. She had a short, narrow, white band above both eyes that gave her an experienced look. She was five years old, which put her in the typically "middle-aged" group according to the rest of her clan. A formidable predatory animal if ever there was one.

What had happened to them – she thought. Why had her more than forty-six thousand brother and sister spotted hyenas sunk to the low of becoming universally known as the scavengers and thieves of the plains? In reality, they were not the gluttonous, stupid, or foolish animals some believed them to be. Hera supposed that a few of them could be described as such, but this was not the brand that she wanted to portray or be a part of. She believed passionately that the spotted hyena genus was a highly successful animal group and predator, able to adapt easily to changing circumstances and quickly take any advantageous opportunities that came their way. Hera also knew that they were primarily hunters and not scavengers. Many of them would run through herds of prey in order to select specific individuals to chase. And chase them they did, sometimes for several miles and at speeds of up to forty miles per hour, before eventually catching and killing the targets. The greater animal community needed to perceive them as the solutions provider rather than the general problems initiator.

Hera was the mother of two healthy and strong, fully weaned, one-year-old cubs—a female (Aphrodite) and a male (Hercules). It was unusual to have two such hale and hearty youngsters from the same litter, but their father had been a fine specimen, and this had probably accounted for it. There had been another male cub born in the same litter, but the two stronger cubs had ganged up on it and had performed neonatal fratricide before they were a month old. The father had just been a sperm donor to Hera, and he had moved on immediately afterward, not being expected, nor required to have any further responsibility toward the family to come.

Hera realized that within her forty-five-member clan (which included fifteen cubs), there was no overt or formalized hierarchical group structure, even though they used a communal den that encouraged a form of social life. There were no rules or guidelines to unite them in what was further required for them to operate more efficiently. They were a compact group, but were not as closely knit as was the ultimate African predator, and the hyena's major competitor, the African wild dog.

Hera knew instinctively that hyenas had to change from being seen as the scavengers of the savanna to a very important segment of the plains food industry if they wanted to improve their survival chances. Spotted hyenas needed to become a trusted brand. She knew that this would not be a simple task because of the openly competitive, rather than cooperative, culture that existed within her own clan. But they had to start somewhere, and it might as well be with her leading the charge from the center. They needed to become very creative in their thinking.

So how to do it? She decided to formalize and itemize everything that she understood about her genus to enable the brand strategy.

The major problem hyenas had was that 50 percent of the times that they made a kill, lions would come along and rob them of their booty. This relegated the hyenas to becoming demoralized watchers, waiting sometimes hours for the lions to finish eating before retrieving the leftovers for themselves.

This activity must not to be allowed to continue. A solution to the problem was necessary. The clan had to understand what market niche they needed to target and service, and that they then needed to go and capture it, whatever the cost. She asked herself the following questions:

Firstly – what was it that spotted hyenas do best? In functional terms, of all the African carnivores, they make the most efficient use of all animal matter, having the capacity to digest everything, including *all* meat, bone, and skin. They also show great flexibility in their hunting and foraging—that is, they can hunt alone, in small parties of two to six individuals, or in larger groups.

Secondly – what type of prey could hyenas successfully hunt that their main competitors (lions) would eat if presented to them? Elephants, buffalo, and giraffes would be specifically avoided as being too big for the hyenas to kill. Therefore zebras, wildebeests, kudu, impalas, and springbok, with weights ranging from 700 pounds to 120 pounds, would then be the foods of choice. If one animal in the above categories was targeted for a kill and left for the lions, then a second and third kill could be made for the hyenas themselves, and the lions would probably leave the rest of the hyenas' kills alone.

Next, Hera thought through how this strategy might be implemented. It had to be done simply, in a straightforward manner, and be easily understood by all the clan members as well as by their competitors. It would also need to be understood by the prey animals, so that they appreciated the overall game that they were involved in. The savanna required a stable market in which every animal understood how and in what form their share took in the rewards to which everyone contributed. They had to know as much about their market and their competition, as they knew about themselves. The solution was to become a very efficient, low-cost, quality provider, which should result in a win-win for all those involved.

In order to become a recognizable brand, however, the hyenas had to earn and gain the reputation of being a trusted, predictable, consistent, and quality supplier of the products that they would be offering to and taking from the community.

Well, Hera reflected, this is how they would do it:

- A hunt with a minimum of three kills by the hyenas would be undertaken every second day, with the objective of leaving the first kill for the lions and then keeping the balance for themselves. Feeding the lions would always take first priority. She knew that this "thinking out of the box" strategy would be a hard sell to the rest of the clan, but she also knew that something both radical and innovative had to be done if their ultimate goal of survival was to be achieved.
- Every other day an investigation would be done to confirm where the lions were and to establish if there were any prey herds in close proximity to them (say within a five-mile radius). They also needed to ascertain the number of older, younger, injured, and weaker animals that were in these herds and identify those as the potential targets.

Each investigation day would take the following formal format. The clan would wake up a half hour before dawn and suckle any cubs that needed feeding until sunup. All clan members would then have a dust bath to ensure that they all looked clean, well groomed, and presentable for that day, engendering a feeling of team and self-pride. All of the smaller cubs not old enough to accompany the investigative groups in their quests would then be taken back to the communal den by five designated females whose responsibility was to protect them from any predators during the day.

Two investigation groups would then be made up of four hunting packs of six hyenas each, and all of these would leave in different directions forty-five minutes after sunup. The highest-ranking hyena in seniority and experience would lead each group. She would be the strategist responsible for maintaining discipline and ensuring that the protocols would be followed. Each of the groups would spend the rest of the morning and early afternoon investigating where the lions and the prey herds were. One hour before sundown that evening, they would return to the den for a liaison meeting of all group leaders.

The hunt-and-kill day following would have a slightly different format. The clan would wake up a half hour before sunup, suckle the cubs, have a dust bath, and go back to the den. After this, a single, large hunting pack of twenty-five members would assemble, and all of the participants would vocalize the *who-oop* call for a full minute, which would let any nearby lions and prey know that the hyenas were going on the hunt. They would then leave for the previous evening's agreed to and pre-assigned targeted herd. The hunting group would kill an animal and leave it for the lions. They would then kill at least two more animals for themselves, which they would dine on. Meat would be taken back to the den for the guardian mothers and for all older meat-eating cubs.

Hera passionately believed that this change would have the dramatic effect of using their core competencies of flexibility and adaptability to ensure and improve the prospects of the spotted hyena's long-term presence and survival. This, in a world that was becoming more cunning, more competitive, and more demanding day by day, would also earn the lions' respect for the hyenas as being committed suppliers.

That afternoon, Hera discussed her ideas separately with the five other senior clan matriarchs, and a full clan meeting was scheduled for later in the day at the den. By sundown, all thirty adult clan members had arrived, and Hera put forward her proposal to them in the simplest way that she knew how. During her talk, there were the usual grumbling sounds and mutterings from some of the longer serving members, asking why they should change when things were reasonably comfortable and sufficient with the status quo. However, the majority younger group agreed strongly with the changes that were sure to bring them many advantages and excitement. They seemed excited by the idea of hyenas becoming a more respected group in the savanna.

Hera took a number of questions at the end, and a large majority voted in the proposal. The clan's senior matriarchs then adjourned together to put the new structures and logistics into place, believing there was no time to proceed like the present. They would start implementing the new strategy the following day.

The new company Hyena Habitat was born, and the proof of the pudding was seen in the eating successes that followed.

LEADERS DO WHAT IS RIGHT RATHER THAN WHAT IS POPULAR.

CHAPTER 6

"Do not blame God for having created the lion, but thank him for not having given it wings."
—OLD ETHIOPIAN PROVERB

A CLEAR TALE

The Wild Ass and the Lion
A Modified Aesop's Fable

A wild ass and a lion entered into an alliance so that they might capture the beasts of the forest with greater ease. The lion agreed to assist the wild ass with his strength, while the wild ass gave the lion the benefit of his greater speed. When they had taken as many beasts as their necessities required, the lion undertook to distribute the prey, and for this purpose divided them into three shares.

"I will take the first share," he said, "because I am king. And also the second share, as I am your partner in the chase. And the third share—believe me—will be a source of great evil to you unless you willingly resign it to me and set off as fast as you can."

Might makes right. Beware.

ZEBRA ZOOLOGY

No animal in nature has a more distinctive and recognizable coat than the African zebra. A zebra's black-and-white coat is unique to each animal and primarily for camouflage. When zebras are attempting to escape predators, the patterns together with the crisscrossing running actions of the animals make it difficult for the predators to identify and target individuals. Also, the uniqueness of the striping gives the added advantage of assisting zebras in recognizing one another.

Zebron was standing on a slightly elevated flat rock near the center of the 175-square-mile Matobo National Park in southeastern Zimbabwe, close to the Botswana border. The general scenic view that he was taking in of the park was a range of domes, spires, and balancing rock formations that had been hewn out of the solid granite plateau through millions of years of erosion and weathering. The dawn light was starting to flash through the surrounding trees, piercing the area with darting and beautiful colors accompanied by the shadows that were brought along with it.

Zebras are animals that exist in small family groups called harems. Each harem consists of a stallion, three or four mares, and their young. These harems generally combine with other harems to form larger herds, which can then number in the hundreds. Herds of zebras all graze on grass together, family members remaining close within the herd's boundaries. Within these large groups, each animal contributes its eyes and ears to being alert to the dangers of predators – and there are many.

Zebron was a twelve-year-old Burchell's zebra stallion. He stood sixty inches tall at the shoulder and weighed a lean 820 pounds. He exuded the confident presence that a good leader should exude, and he was standing facing an assembly of eleven other impeccably turned-out zebra stallions.

"Thank you for coming," Zebron said to the group. "I called this meeting today in response to concerns expressed by a majority of you regarding the unprecedented and unacceptable number of predatory losses that we have been experiencing lately. It is quite evident that our major predators—lions, cheetahs, and hyenas—have reengineered their hunting strategies of late, and we are suffering badly as a result. We are a herd of ninety-five at present, and we have seen our numbers diminish due to predation by roughly one every three days for the last three months. This cannot be allowed to continue, and we must come up with an effective counterstrategy. This extremely high cost of doing business will eventually force our herd into extinction if we are not very careful. So my question to you all is—what can we do about it? In saying this, I would now like to open up the floor for discussion, and I ask for your input please."

Zambon, a relatively tall stallion with good stature and a well-groomed mane, was the first to step forward. He said, "Over the last month, I have lost two mares and two foals from my harem, and I am bitterly ashamed by this. We need a much more effective early warning system to let us know when predators are around. How can we do this?"

The zebra fraternity knew that they basically served as a food source in the savanna and that they would have some predatory losses regardless of what they did to reduce losses. Additionally, other deaths occurred due to old age, accidents, or the environment. What they had to do was to absolutely minimize their overall total losses in order to guarantee their survival.

Zebron answered Zambon after a few seconds of reflection. "I have been in contact with a group of vervet monkeys led by a very astute individual by the name of Vivo. If we zebras find it acceptable,

Vivo has committed his troop to us to become our extra eyes and ears on a full-time basis, guaranteeing someone to watch for and warn us early of potential predators. All we would have to do in return is to allow his members to ride on our backs when we move from one area to the next. They would do this for an initial one-year trial period, with further extensions to be negotiated. We would form a partnership with them where we would be totally committed to one another. Remember that a partnership is as close as a marriage, and this would be a win-win situation for both of our species."

Braying assent broke out from the assembled audience, signifying acceptance and approval of what had just been proposed. Details would, however, have to be sorted out.

Zoresh, another male, stood up on his hind legs, raising his front hooves to indicate his desire to be the next to be heard. Neighing shrilly, he said, "I have an idea that might help us further. Why do we not encourage more wildebeests to join us in our herd, and instead of having the present ratio with them of approximately one to one, we try to increase the ratio to at least one and a half to one or higher of wildebeests to zebras—that way there is a better likelihood of one of the wildebeests being taken in preference to one of us. Also if we ensure that the wildebeests feed at the extreme edges of our grazing areas, this will again give a better likelihood of one of them being taken in preference to one of us who would be well inside that perimeter." There was again loud braying assent from the group.

Zamphir, a seven-year-old harem leader, piped up next. "There are quite a few of us who have become fat and slow, allowing the predators to run us down more easily. We need to choose to become generally healthier, eat a more nutritious diet, and get into better shape. We need to be able to increase our speeds above that of the wildebeests, again giving a better likelihood of them being taken before us. We must become lean and mean." There was a general nodding of heads at the end of these words. It was quite clear that the wildebeests were to become a very important tool in the zebras' strategy for survival.

"Well," said Zebron, "it seems that we have three strategies here—the Vervet-Monkey Strategy, the Wildebeest Strategy, and the Physical Strategy. I will personally take responsibility for implementing the Vervet-Monkey Strategy. Zoresh will be responsible for increasing the wildebeest numbers and their placements. Zamphir will ensure that the physical training for becoming lean and mean gets carried out by all of us. We will set a time limit of sixty days for total completion, which, to my mind, is a feasible goal. We must understand, however, that our very survival hinges on how successful we are in achieving these goals, and we must commit one hundred percent of our efforts to succeed. Please give your unequivocal support. Are there any questions? Are we all agreed?"

Zebron paused and then went on. "Seeing there are no questions and if we are all agreed, let us implement and meet again after the sixty-day period for a review."

The group quietly filed out of the meeting area and immediately started work on the new strategies.

At the sixty-day review meeting, it was noted that good progress had been made in all three strategies. The status of the Vervet-Monkey Strategy was that at any one time there were at least twenty vervet monkey guards in close proximity to the herd and early warnings from them had resulted in at least twenty-five attacks on the herd by predators becoming unsuccessful. A great result!

With the Wildebeest Strategy it was noted that one herd of blue- and one herd of black-wildebeest had joined up with the zebra herd and for the first time more wildebeest than zebra had been taken by predators during the sixty day trial period. More wildebeest were to be encouraged in to swell and meet the numbers required.

The Physical Strategy seemed to be lagging though as only 65 percent of qualifying zebras had undertaken the required activities. More effort was needed to be made in this regard.

A satisfying result nonetheless.

A LEADER HOLDS ACCOUNTABLE THOSE WHO WORK WITH HIM.

CHAPTER 7

"Courage is almost a contradiction in terms. It means a strong desire to live taking the form of a readiness to die."
—G. K. CHESTERTON

A TALE OF UNDERSTANDING

The Hare and the Hound
An Aesop's Fable

A hound startled a hare from its lair but, after a long run, gave up the chase.

A hyena, seeing the hound stop, mocked him, saying, "The little one is the best runner of the two."

The hound replied, "You do not see the difference between us: I was only running for a dinner, but the hare was running for his life."

LYCAON PICTUS PACK

The date was December 14, the time 5:09 a.m. The sun was once again preparing to lift itself from below the eastern horizon and offer the guarantee of life to the many thousands of animal inhabitants of the African savanna, as it had done every day for millions of years. Nature's plan for the next fourteen hours was very clear: open skies and blistering heat with temperatures reaching 110°F in the shade—when there was not much shade around. Animals were beginning to wake up and move about.

Yet another dry and hot day promised for the poor inhabitants of Mother Earth. The sun would scorch to a virtual crisp anything that was too stupid or too foolish not to get out of its blistering rays and not move into any shade protection. The weather had not changed in three months, and the arid, cracked ground was at its most desperate. There was not a breath of wind to disturb the languidly dancing heat waves that were already rising from the parched, brown earth. The only sound that broke the deafening silence was a soft, questioning, whine, followed by a second, a third, and finally a seventh whine—all with different pitches. The children were hungry. They demanded nourishment, just like the blood-red sand beneath their padded feet demanded nourishment, too.

Sasha, the matriarch and leader of the pack, stood up slowly to her full thirty inch height and very deliberately stretched her long, delicately muscled legs one at a time, all the while keeping her eyes focused on the rest of her team, including those little ones. The time had come for them to depart this relatively comfortable place and move on. She had a foreboding that if they did not make this change soon, they would all be doomed to die an excruciating and hungry death. All of the smaller antelope had moved on to other areas, and the food pickings had become sparse and not very nourishing.

Sasha reflected for a time on where she and her pack were. It was in the Hluhluwe-iMfolozi Park in South Africa which comprises three hundred and seventy square miles of undulating and hilly topography made up of both wide and deep valleys. It is fortunate to have a rich wildlife, being home to more than one hundred animal species including all of the big game animals. It sustains large populations of lions, rhinos, wildebeests, hyenas, warthogs, and impalas. This was the survival battleground for Sasha and her *Lycaon pictus* clan.

Sasha walked over to Jinx, the group's alpha male. She nuzzled his neck, and he looked quizzically up at her. Sasha and Jinx had been together for six years as devoted partners, with the last five of those six years serving as the senior alpha duo of their clan. Despite her years in the leadership role, Sasha had not become tired of ensuring the clan's survival. She was just as dedicated to the task as she had been at the beginning. The pack had changed slightly over time. Some of them had grown old and passed on naturally; some had been killed by predators; and a few had lost their lives due to stupidity during the hunt despite Sasha's and Jinx's best efforts. Those members that had survived and remained, were the ones not yet ready to give up on this life and were totally focused on the cause—the survival of their species.

The current team was strong both in number and resolve. It comprised eight adults and ten pups, with all the adults totally committed and determined to attain their united goal. It had not been an easy six years with many battles being fought and won, yet the war for survival never ended. Losing was however, never considered an option.

As Sasha nudged Jinx to his feet, she reflected on the time when things were different from what they were now. Food had been plentiful then. Sasha had been born into the Hondo clan—a group of twenty members. They were a beautiful subset of their genus who embraced the accolade of being recognized by their competitors and peers in the savanna as being the role model killing machines of the African predator fraternity. It was Sasha's and Jinx's calling to lead, and lead they had. Sasha had been the second born in her litter in a family of six other siblings, with her being one of only two females. Her brothers had been tough on her, and she had educated herself very early in what was needed to defend herself from those wanting to either beat her up, or break her down. She had assimilated those life-defensive necessary skills and had improved on them every day, recalling continually into her mind's memory her eldest brother's comments: "Sasha, you will never remain alive if you cower and give up before a rival or an enemy." She had taken this advice to heart, and she cowered no more. She had learned how to hunt, how to strike on cue, and how to kill. She did not take pleasure in the actual action of the killing of an animal prey, but the death was always quick and the rewards satisfying.

What was her final claim to fame? She was an extremely proud, seventy-five pound

AFRICAN WILD DOG!

An African wild dog on its own is a tough and agile predator, but a pack of African wild dogs is a singular force of nature. They achieve this status by using teamwork and strategy. It is only by diligently studying the battlefield, directing the game plan, and analyzing the moves that a collection of these canines then become an elite predatory unit, absolutely respected by all of those threatened by them.

Sasha had been taught very early on that African wild dogs do not kill their prey as most other competitor predators do – by suffocation. Wild dogs are too small and too light in weight to hold down an antelope by clamping their teeth on its throat or over its nose as a lion or a cheetah would. They have to do something else, but it is that something that gets their name tarnished and defiled. They always attack as a team, and they then tear the prey limb from limb as quickly as they can to ensure that it does not get away. Usually this dismembering terminates the animal's life very quickly due to its rapid blood loss. The clan prided itself in its efficiency being seen as one of its core competencies.

Many animals argue that this type of killing is brutal and savage, but the critics fail to understand the physics of their being dogs. Despite the bad publicity, this was their brand. Sasha knew that they were *the* most successful predators on the African plains with a more than 75 percent kill rate of all targeted animals. She also knew that in order to ensure her clan's survival, they all had to be totally committed to maintaining this minimum efficiency level every single day of their lives.

As in most well run businesses, not all of the wild dog pack takes part in actual hunting. Some, both males and females, stay behind to look after and educate the pups, and are responsible for defending the den if attacked. Some stay behind because they have no choice in the matter - older dogs and those with injuries or impairments would only hinder the hunt and possibly get further injured, or perhaps even killed, if they tried to help. The ones behind awaited the spoils, and the pack *always* delivered.

Sasha nudged Jinx one more time and whispered in his ear, "Let's go!"

While walking together with Jinx back to the den, Sasha thought a bit more about her pack's history and what had brought them success over the years. She knew that to have a strong team ethos, a strong leadership, and a strong belief in what was possible was extremely important in the battle for life.

The dogs were generally better known across the bushveld by their recognized scientific brand name *Lycaon pictus* which literally translated means "painted wolf." They have mottled brown and patchy coats and a tail with a white tip, with no two dogs showing exactly the same markings, making it easy to identify individuals within the group. The dogs have excellent vision, a lean build, and relative to their size, a stronger bite than any other carnivore on earth. Sasha knew that these attributes helped immensely toward achieving their goal of very efficient survival.

African wild dogs hunt in very committed teams in accordance with well-established tactics and patterns. When chasing prey, their strategy is to run in single file, and when the leading dog becomes weary, it moves to run as the back marker of the line and bring up the rear. This requires the next dog at the front of the line to then take the lead and to continue setting the needed chasing pace.

Other core competencies of African wild dogs and which they continually improve on, are their instinctive sense of resolve, their communication skills, and their ability to work as a close-knit team where all understand completely their roles and responsibilities. Once they have decided on a target, they will chase it for hours on end to achieve the kill. They simply run their prey ragged until it stops attempting to flee and allows the dogs to strike.

Once a kill is made, the pack allows the youngest dogs to eat first, followed by the most senior dogs, and finally the balance of the group is allowed to eat. The reason for this is twofold: it ensures the growth and the strength of the younger dogs for the future, and it keeps the rest of the pack hungry and motivated to improve their performance in the following day's hunt. This activity is in strict contrast to their competitors' (lions and hyenas) actions when dealing with a kill, which generally takes the form of a free-for-all gorging led by the most powerful member of the group.

Sasha reflected on her clan's success to date of being the "top dogs" in the predator survival race and how this culture could be consistently encouraged and established to ensure their continued success into the future. As their leader, she realized that the following points were extremely important to their survival:

- The leader must be honest, have absolute integrity, and be specific in her expectations.
- The leader does what is right for the pack.
- The leader must not be afraid of confrontation or challenges.

- The leader is always full of praise for jobs well done and makes others in the pack better.
- The leader is always growing.
- The pack must avoid being the hunted rather than being the hunters.
- The pack must choose its prey very carefully (e.g., type of antelope) and the terrain that it inhabits (preferably hilly).
- The pack must be very creative and able to change tactics while on the move.
- The pack must constantly train, train, and train some more—all team members must be on the same wavelength at all times.
- They must be creative and encourage the element of surprise.
- They must bring in new blood to guarantee succession and protect the next generation at all costs.

Sasha knew that the pack had to act as a single unit, being single-minded and single-purposed. Success would only continue with a perfected formula of instinct, skill, experience, and strategy. Hunting together efficiently would enable them to adjust as the game board changed, allowing them to reap their just rewards. The fight for survival would never end. They would *never* relinquish their number-one status in the savanna. She knew she was a good leader. She also knew that she must not become complacent in her leadership and must always be on the lookout for new ways of doing things. She wanted the business of Lycaon Pictus Pack to continue on indefinitely into the future.

Sasha playfully nudged Jinx again and said louder this time, "Let's go and rally the pack!"

LEADERS ARE POSSESSED BY THEIR DREAMS.

CHAPTER 8

"The bitterest tears shed over graves are for words left unsaid and deeds left undone."
—*HARRIET BEECHER STOWE*

THE TEAM TALE

The Kingdom of the Lion
An Aesop's Fable

When the lion reigned over the beasts of the earth, he was never cruel or tyrannical, but as gentle and just as a king ought to be. During his reign, he called a general assembly of the beasts and drew up a code of laws under which all were to live in perfect equality and harmony. The wolf and the lamb, the tiger and the stag, the leopard and the kid, the dog and the hare—all should dwell side by side in unbroken peace and friendship. The hare said, "Oh! How I have longed for this day when the weak take their place without fear by the side of the strong!"

SURVIVE-OR-DIE
ANIMAL CONVENTION

It was another blisteringly hot day in the African bushveld, with the lazy breeze coming in from the northeast. This wind was a sign of an impending two- to three-day wet period, which would generally start within twenty-four hours.

The area of the bushveld where the meeting was being held was ideal for its purpose. It was a section of grassland of approximately three-quarters of an acre in size, and it was completely encircled by a fairly dense forested area of at least a mile in width in all directions before it met up with rivers, hills, and grassland savannas. This central piece of grassland was like an oasis in a desert.

The time was 9:55 a.m., and the formal part of the meeting was due to start at 10:00 a.m. and go on for as long as it took.

Sitting in a structured circle around the center of the meeting area were two lions, two elephants, three cheetahs, two baboons, two hyenas, three zebras—each with an attached vervet-monkey attendant—and two African wild dogs.

Precisely at ten, Eliva, one of the elephants, drew herself up to her full height and trumpeted loudly to signify that the formal part of the meeting was now open.

Genghis, the larger of the two lions, sat up straight and started speaking just loudly enough so that the rest of the attendees could hear him clearly over the African white-noise hum in the background.

"Thank you all for coming. I know that some of you have traveled unbelievably long distances to be here with us today at this neutral venue in the area known as Chobe National Park, but we lions sincerely believe that the very survival of the African animal kingdom is at stake and that intense discussions are needed by major stakeholders to address this, and we lions sincerely appreciate your being here. There have been incredible changes for the worse to our traditional habitats during the last one hundred years, and we species who are here today, as well as those species who are not here today, are all threatened with eventual complete and total extinction by these changes that are taking place at a terrifying rate."

Genghis continued. "First and foremost, before we begin the formal discussions session of the meeting, I would like to confirm unequivocally of our absolute commitment to one another of complete safety from each another during the time that we are here until the time that we are back with our loved ones. So please feel free to have one-on-one personal discussions between species in full confidence of safety. Without this, we cannot have the absolutely civilized and urgent discussions that are needed here today to ensure the animal kingdom's survival."

"Having said this," Genghis carried on, "I would like to open the meeting with an introduction and a setting of the stage.

"There always has been a reasonably robust and beneficial balance in nature that we animals have understood and followed religiously. This depended and was based on a generally long-term, stable surrounding environment. For example, we lions would restrict our birthrate so as not to deplete our prey's numbers, thus ensuring a balance between supply and demand. If we had not done this, we would have been faced with a catch-22 situation of selfish survival with more lions taking more buffalo, with buffalo then having to breed more than normal just to maintain their numbers, thus requiring more grassland for themselves. This would have led to the elephants and antelope having less volume of food stock available to them, encouraging starvation and sickness, and allowing them to be more easily taken by lions, leopards, cheetahs, and others, in a spiral to eventual extinction of all of us," said Genghis.

"Also, zebras, such as Zebron here, would probably have had to range more widely in search of grazing and cross more rivers, thus becoming more susceptible to attacks by crocodiles. It goes on and on," said Genghis.

"Unfortunately, times have changed dramatically. The overriding threat to our existence has become the human species, which I do not consider to be part of nature. Humans have an incredible greed for everything, whether it moves or does not move, as well as an insatiable thirst for energy. They are destroying our habitats and eliminating us at an incredible rate by way of poisonous pollution that affects the climate. Thus, the scenario that I painted a few minutes ago is now becoming a reality.

"The humans also poach, hunt, and kill us for sport for our skins, tusks, horns, heads, teeth, and anything else that they can sell. We have to realize that we are in a war, and the humans are a common predator and enemy of ours. Since we here all recognize this, we must make plans and concerted efforts together to counter their threat. This is the reason we are all here today—to discuss what we can do about them. Unity will be our strength in this endeavor.

"As far as each of our species is concerned, the independent survival strategies that we have each developed for ourselves and shared among one another yesterday should be acted on by each of us with immediate effect. The details could perhaps one day be compiled in some way to be shared and understood by all of the world's species. We all have to accept and respect these considered strategies as being very personal, and the best solutions for each of us," Genghis said. "This concludes my opening statement. After our break for lunch, I would like to invite each delegation to address the rest of us and give us their thoughts and proposals regarding this human threat, starting with the elephants. I would now like to call an adjournment until twelve."

The group reconvened at noon with the individual presentations carrying on until seven that evening. This was thus the First African Animal Convention, themed "Survive or Die," with the main thrust targeted at the very real, more global, human threats that had not been specifically addressed in each of the species's individual strategies for survival.

After a general summation of the proceedings and with four resolutions being made, the convention closed at eight. Each group then started to make its way back home with the words "Survive or Die" first and foremost in their thoughts.

It was a start.

Signed:
Genghis (*Panthera leo*)
AD October 20XX

LEADERS TAKE RESPONSIBILITY FOR WHAT THEY DO.

CHAPTER 9

"The perils of animal hunting are great—especially for the animal."
—*IVAN SCOTT (WITH APOLOGIES TO WALTER CRONKITE)*

A SAD TALE

The Hart and the Hunter
An Aesop's Fable

The hart was once drinking from a pool and admiring the noble figure he made there. "Ah," said he, "where can you see such noble horns as these, with such antlers! I wish I had legs more worthy to bear such a noble crown; it is a pity they are so slim and slight."

At that moment, a hunter approached and sent an arrow whistling after him. Away bounded the hart, and soon, by the aid of his nimble legs, he was nearly out of sight of the hunter. But not noticing where he was going, he passed under some trees with branches growing low down in which his antlers got caught, so that the hunter had time to come up. "Alas! Alas!" cried the hart. "We often despise what is most useful to us."

SAFARIS UNLIMITED

"**C**ome on, Jonas. We have to be ready for the customer by the time he arrives today. I need you to pick him up at noon at the airport in Maun, helicopter him back here, and get him comfortably settled in his suite so that he can be ready for tomorrow's experiences." These were the words of John Jones, the company's owner, head ranger, and chief personal game guide.

"The company" and "here" was Safaris Unlimited's ultra-luxurious private game lodge situated on Chief's Island, the largest island in the Okavango Delta in Botswana. "Tomorrow's experiences" were the activities that were planned for the customer, which included the trophy hunting and killings of a Shinde male lion, a Bedwe buffalo, and a well-tusked migrant African elephant. Safaris Unlimited had never undertaken these illegal activities before, but the customer had offered $10,000 for each trophy bagged. This was over and above the normal and very high daily costs charged. Jones had become greedy when negotiating this offer and had readily agreed to supply this "new product" for the proffered money. The "customer" was a very wealthy businessman from eastern Europe who had promised not to breathe a word to a soul about these extra activities in his safari. He was tight on schedule and had only two days to secure his kills and leave.

Unfortunately, Jones hadn't thought out the plan's execution very well, and the undertaking did not go according to expectations. The hired helicopter that had been arranged to fly the customer to the lodge and which was also to be used as transport to the animal areas arrived at the Maun Airport an hour late, and its engine refused to start again once the customer was on board. This resulted in a panicky scrambling around to hire a Land Rover as alternative transport to the lodge, which led to a very uncomfortable five-and-a-half-hour drive, with arrival in the dark. The not-very-happy customer was then settled into his suite and treated to the sumptuous meal and drinks as had been originally planned.

The next morning, the helicopter arrived at the lodge one hour after sunup (again, a half hour late). The customer, the guides, and two brand-new CZ 416 Rigby scoped hunting rifles were loaded on board the helicopter, and they left for the Shinde area of the Delta. After a relatively short flight, they touched down on an open piece of grassland near the area where they expected the Shinde lions to be relaxing. Unfortunately for the hunters, the pride had moved on the previous day after hearing a rumor of the arrival of potential human predators, and no one could locate the lions from the ground. Additionally, no lions were seen during a one-hour circuit by the helicopter, which came back to the temporary operations base so the company could hold a planning and strategy meeting. The expedition thus started disastrously for both Safaris Unlimited and the customer, without a lion trophy being bagged.

Just after lunch that afternoon, a thunderstorm of unimaginable power suddenly erupted and raged for two hours in the area where the hunters were stationed, leading to mild local flooding. The group did get soaking wet, however, which led to the rest of the day's intended agenda of shooting a buffalo also being canceled. They finally flew back to the lodge to change clothes and dry off. A day had been wasted. The customer was not happy. However, there was always the following day for the elephant.

The next morning arrived, beautifully clear, with the promise of a sunny day, and after an early luxurious breakfast, all the necessary equipment, guides, guns, and customer were again loaded into the helicopter. It took off and they settled down for the hour-and-a-bit flight to the Thaoge River, where the elephants were reported to be.

After a very scenic but uneventful flight, the helicopter arrived above the general vicinity where the elephants had previously been observed. After flying a series of ever widening circles, they found them! A group of twelve elephants of varying sizes and ages were feeding in a reasonably dense area of bush a mile west of a major bend in the Thaoge River, and about ten miles north of where they were last reported as having been seen two days previously. There was intense excitement inside the helicopter after spotting the elephants, with the customer shouting and screaming out his delight at the prospect of the shoot.

Jones immediately ordered the helicopter pilot to land in a small clearing that they had flown over, which was about three-quarters of a mile southeast of where the elephants were positioned. It was a perfect area for landing, so they did, in a cloud of African dust. The group quickly disembarked. Jones gave orders to the pilot to stay with the helicopter and one of the two guides was instructed to make up a rudimentary camp for the day under a nearby acacia tree. Jones, the customer, and the other guide would be back at the camp for celebration in about four hours' time. Replete with the two CZ 416 rifles and sufficient ammunition in cross-over body belts, the trio then left to go and do the deed.

The bush vegetation was fairly dense on the trek to where the elephants were, and the journey took all of forty minutes. It certainly did not help matters that the customer was grossly overweight and had to stop and rest for at least one minute out of every five that they slowly walked. Finally, they saw them. The animals were in deep under-growth, stripping the surrounding trees of food to as high a level as they could reach with their fully extended trunks. The bush was so thick that the hunters could partially see only one or two elephants at any one time without moving substantially to the left or to the right. This was not going to be an easy kill.

Jones started guiding the customer to find a position from where a clear shot could possibly be taken. This was not a simple task, again due to the denseness of the bush, the customer's size, and the customer's excitement level. Two things that Jones did not know about his customer (but should have) were firstly that he did not take advice or instruction readily and secondly that he had never shot such a powerful rifle before in his life. This proved to be a recipe for disaster.

The hunters chose a seventy-five-yard-distant shooting position away from the foraging elephants, and a fully grown but still reasonably juvenile bull with a fairly large set of tusks became the target animal. It was not going to be an easy or clear shot due to the thick undergrowth in the first place, but they would also have to wait a short while to see if a clearer shot could be taken, which would give a better result. The customer, his hands shaking with anticipation, did not position the gun very snugly into his shoulder, so when the shot did come, the barrel jumped up, the rifle kicked back, and the customer fell over backwards. The bullet went through a fleshy part of the elephant's ear rather than through his brain as was the intention. It caused virtually no damage.

Pandemonium ensued as the twelve elephants seemed to know exactly what had just happened and from where the bullet had originated. They, as one, immediately charged at the customer. He attempted to run back in the direction of the helicopter, but the huge matriarch caught up with him and gored him to death with her enormous tusks against a tree. The balance of the elephants then thundered past, trumpeting and snorting, and trampling to death both Jones and the second guide while on their way to the clearing where the helicopter was parked.

The elephants quickly arrived at the clearing and, not stopping for breath, charged the helicopter and upended it, smashing it into small pieces. The temporary campsite was also destroyed and everything found there was strewn onto the ground. After about a half hour of snorting, trumpeting and stomping everything in sight, all the elephants turned around and disappeared into the thicket in the direction from where they had come. The helicopter pilot and the remaining guide were nowhere to be seen. It was going to be a long and dangerous walk home for them.

Eliva turned to Kalifa just before re-entering the undergrowth and said, "Mufta was lucky today, but that was a terrific win for us animals. This was a good start!"

A LEADER REACTS TO HIS OWN FAILURES AND ACKNOWLEDGES THEM.

Bibliography

Hacker, Stephen, and Marvin Washington. *Leading Peak Performance: Lessons from the Wild Dogs of Africa.* Milwaukee, USA: ASQ Quality Press, 2007.

Musicbank Limited. *Wildlife Diary: 12 DVD Collector's Edition.* DVD. Norfolk, UK: Musicbank Limited, 2004.

National Geographic Television and Film. *The Pack: Wild Dogs and Lions.* DVD. Washington, DC: NGHT Inc., 2009.

National Geographic."Baboon"2015 http//animals. nationalgeographic.com/animals/mammals/ baboon

National Geographic."Zebra"2015 http//animals. nationalgeographic.com/animals/mammals/ zebra

National Geographic."Hyena"2015 http//animals. nationalgeographic.com/animals/mammals/ hyena

Wikipedia. "Hluhluwe-iMfolozi Park" June 2015 https// en.wikipedia.org/wiki/Hluhluwe_iMfolozi_Park

Wikipedia. "Kruger National Park" May 2015 https// en.wikipedia.org/wiki/Kruger_National_Park

Wikipedia. "Okavango Delta" May 2015 https// en.wikipedia.org/wiki/Okavango_Delta

Wikipedia. "Matobo National Park" June 2015 https/ en.wikipedia.org/wiki/Matobo_National_Park

Wikipedia. "Sabi Sand Game Reserve" May 2015 https// en.wikipedia.org/wiki/Sabi_Sand_Game_Reserve

Wikipedia. "Chobe National Park" March 2015 https// en.wikipedia.org/wiki/Chobe_National_Park

World Wildlife Fund. "Adopt a Lion" 2015 http:// www.worldwildlife.org/ species/lion

World Wildlife Fund. "Adopt an Elephant" 2015 http://www.worldwildlife.org/ species/elephant

World Wildlife Fund. "Adopt a Cheetah" 2015 http://www.worldwildlife.org/ species/cheetah

World Wildlife Fund. "Adopt an African Wild Dog" 2015 http://www.worldwildlife.org/ species/african wild dog

Photographs kindly donated by

- Dudley Morgan (Canada)
- Michael Booth (Canada)
- Nicholas Presland (South Africa)
- Russell Burgess (Canada)